Sarah Caulfield's work is inspired—in the antique sense of the verb *inspirare*, to impart, to instill, to breathe life into. Fully inhabiting the fragility and messiness of ailing bodies and anxious minds, Caulfield probes with surgical ruthlessness and hard-earned empathy into the meat of something that might be called (if this collection did not resist the clichés of universality) the human condition. "Your spine is made of beach glass," a time-traveling woman, speaking "To The Girl I Was," informs her past self. "It will withstand." The same is true of the seventeen spoken-word poems that make up the vertebrae of SPINE. These are stories about pain and compassion, despair and endurance, doubt and faith, that will not "fade in the telling." They will withstand.
—SAMANTHA PIOUS Finalist for the 2015 Charlotte Mew Prize

SPINE stitches together a mythology of sickness, without romanticising it—this is vital, visceral work, grounded in the realities of blood and bone. Glittering fragments of imagery repeat and refract throughout the collection, weaving through a world of sterile hospital walls and incense-rich catholic churches. Here, religion, sex, illness, and death all bleed into each other: themes not isolated but mutually entrenched, and foundational to Caulfield's voice. This complex self-portrait is an assured debut that overwhelms the senses and improves on every reading.
—HEL ROBIN GURNEY nominee for the Rhysling Poetry Award, spoken word performer and scholar (*The Sleeping Princess,* EdFringe, 2016)

Sarah Caulfield's writing is contemporary and engaging. Honest and important. I'm really happy to have a writer like Sarah creating LGBT work that is likely to be read forever; she makes the new writers' landscape much more exciting.
—REMILYN BROWNE OSHIBANJO member of London-based creative collective SXWKS, author of *these are the most terrifying thoughts*

SPINE

SPINE

Sarah Caulfield

HEADMISTRESS PRESS

Copyright © 2017 by Sarah Caulfield
All rights reserved.

ISBN-13: 978-0997914993
ISBN-10: 0997914998

This book may not be reproduced, in whole or in part, including illustrations, in any form (beyond that permitted by Sections 107 and 108 of the U.S. Copyright Law and except by reviewers for the public press), without written permission from the publishers.

Cover art:
Artist: Sonja Sekula (1918 - 1963)
Work title, year: without title, 1942
Technic: oil on canvas
Size: 61 x 96,5 cm
Courtesy Galerie HILT Basel

Cover & book design by Mary Meriam.

PUBLISHER
Headmistress Press
60 Shipview Lane
Sequim, WA 98382
Telephone: 917-428-8312
Email: headmistresspress@gmail.com
Website: headmistresspress.blogspot.com

*To all the lost girls trying to drag themselves home.
The night never lasts.*

Contents

Tallowflesh	1
Chosen One	2
not about anyone you know	3
Here To Recruit You	4
lapsed	5
this is not	6
talk me into going up	7
Rites of Passage	8
Ten Hail Mary's Worth	9
Don't fade in the telling	10
Siren	11
Sweetie	12
Small and Insignificant Confessions	13
Give blood, join Roller Derby	15
Anxiety Attack on Regent Street	16
the last great loves	17
To the Girl I Was:	19
About the Author	23
Acknowledgments	25

Tallowflesh

Three

I think I made you up inside my head. If I did,
You ripped something on your way out. Call it birthing pains.
Call it the cut of the first breath in your lungs. Call it anything that
Exoticises the muddle of my blood on the floor, that mythologises my breath
Sealing like a mausoleum.
Original sin was always never knowing when to stop, sweetheart.

Two

When I was eight, I read multicoloured pocketbooks.
The Lives of the Saints.
The illustrations very blue and clean.
St. Christopher carrying the Christ Child across the river,
The crushing weight reeling his spine near in half.
I wonder if the water was as cold as the eyes in the blue clean illustrations.
In some countries, they let prisoners out to go to church, did you know that?
I don't have to ask if the carrying hurt. Did you notice that?

One

I am counting down to something but the clocks never stop.
The clocks never stop.
They drag us forward with the deadweight of every breath gone before.
It's a wonder we don't choke on it, sweetheart. But then maybe you do.
Maybe you are.
I can't help you. When I was eight, I read multicoloured picturebooks
And when I was eighteen
I listened to the flight attendant with the same devotion of the evangelist.
Always attend to your own oxygen mask first.
That's why I don't ask if it hurts. I already know, sweetheart.
But then nobody asked St. Christopher if he could bear it either.
And that's why,
Why they made him a saint, and I'm tallow enough left.
I would not set myself on fire.
For you, I would not burn.

Chosen One

It's gonna take you by surprise, kid,
carve you out a new spine and tell you you're lucky
as your bones groan over the weight of living
and your eyes burn like it's the third day in hell.
You still got your legs, kid.
You are not wired up to a bed whilst your organs gasp out,
feeling the gurney or the wheelchair rearrange your meat with each jolt.

So shut your mouth and smile,
learn the taste and chant of *it could be worse.*
It's not that severe. At least it's not —
Cleave your suffering into manageable portions and eat it in small bites.

Despair is the snick of needles probing at the bruising of your eyes,
the trickle of papery sweat against your back as you lay down for this one
last god and pray to be healed. When they open your mouth,
let them put the wafer down. Let the glass against your tongue.
Let them lay hands on you whilst you plateau,
adrift in white paint that feels like light and hurts like sand.

And then:
Talk to the receptionist. We'll see you in a year.
Remember to smile on your way out. It could be worse. Don't think about it.
Why are you crying?

After all, we only took a little blood. Your heart will beat it back.

NOT ABOUT ANYONE YOU KNOW

it starts like this:
glitter-slick solidarity, elbows in my ribs in the nightclub
and hysterical laughter loud as a distress flare in the night,
the smear of lipstick on my teeth you rub off,
your thumb in my mouth and your hair in the light,
and the light is good here, it gilds you into an icon
something other and terrible, a martyred saint with a bloody halo
glimmers your skin to cheap gilt
and i wonder if i put my hands on you if it'd come off on me
if i'd be golden by association

it goes wrong like this:
you voice going evasive on the phone, hollering at someone who i don't know
who's that sweetheart and you go *oh just someone* and change the subject
and what can i say to that really what can i say
and you stop smiling when i hand you a cup of tea,
tension ratchets up your spine
so i've stopped trying to trace it with my fingertips
oedipus gouged his eyes out to unsee something terrible but this isn't greece
this is nothing, this happens every day, this is a tragedy in minor key
and it goes *don't leave don't leave don't leave*

Here to Recruit You

They warned you it would end in tears.
They warned you it would end.
You're gonna die, baby. You're gonna die.
You smiled enamel stars, turned your eyes
to the circuit boards all over America
lighting up like beacons, like a call to arms,
lighting up like the start of something,
And you smiled. *So fucking what.*

And outside, there were cardboard placards,
with empty spaces between the words
but no empty spaces on the sidewalk.

And you won't remember this in the morning
but they made you into a golden calf, they sang you
into a psalm, cookie-cutter messiah, God Bless Fordism

And you won't remember this in the morning
but the morning after
they were spitting hellcats who made you immortal
because there had been a man with a gun
(there's always a man with a gun)
and too soon and too fast and a
whole recruited choir couldn't pull back finite time.

The circuit boards lit up louder.
Purple handprints on plate glass.

And you won't remember this in the morning, but they were there
A people, marching through a city with candles,
turning right to avoid the slaughterhouse just in time.

LAPSED

my body is a catholic
a series of transgressions and punishments
the hole in my ribcage echoing with the ave maria
st sebastian the creak in my bones
st bernadette the ache
st jude the blood on my tongue.
i spit it up and say
forgive me.
i am better than this.

it has been two years since my last confession
since i swooned with holy visions bursting faint-white behind my eyes
and when i called, no one answered.
it was not opened when i knocked, so i clawed down the door instead, said
this is my body, this is my blood
this is my everything and i am more than this
this flesh is only borrowed and i
i am the 21 grams of extra weight science can't explain and
i am the grit in my teeth when i stood up from the blow and said
go on. again. i have been to this place before and survived.
drag me to hell. i'll see you in three days' time.

i want to believe, but i can't open my eyes long enough to see the light.

THIS IS NOT
inspired by the work of richard siken

this is not an autobiography
this is not about anyone you know
that girl you saw once, fainting by the roadside?
yeah, that was someone else.
passing resemblance. you know how it goes.
bad architecture isn't uncommon.

this is not an autobiography
because stories take flesh better
and everyone wants the ending that isn't so.
make it so.
give it a moral and sing it to the children at moonlight.
don't stay to watch them cry.

this is not an autobiography
though the red-eyed, red-lipped days are lingering
loud and yowling, greedy for notice.
you never saw them and were never there.
you heard about them later and stitched up something to talk you into place.
this is how we make ourselves requited, hollow against hollow and
this is how we resonate.

this is not an autobiography
for the vast, unyielding nights
unfolding themselves beneath the glimmer of closed eyelids?
you were alone in this and it was quite ordinary.

TALK ME INTO GOING UP

we have written too much about loss;
crystallised the stories into cliches
where every time the phone rings it is always bad news
and no blood test is benign,
where we construct a narrative out of the ridiculous
and pretend the fact we talked about the weather in the funeral car
is something to weep over.

but we have not said how it comes down to a series of cheap moments;
we have never spoken of how we sat in the basement after our mother rushed
upstairs to the deathbed,
blood-close in our solidarity of the unknown,
sick with awareness we now knew how the story ended.
we sat there for hours but later we found out it had been only minutes,
each waiting for the other to buckle.
loss is sitting in a room hiding from the dead man upstairs
because until you see it can stay fiction.
i was the oldest, so of course i went first; and you would not leave me behind.

Rites of Passage

I don't want to be an adult
I long for eternal nineteen
the golden apple age at which all I have to do is pluck
that appleseed edge of desperation, keen to be liked,
and the churning nausea of a body that sprouts and groans
becomes and begins anew against my will

In ten years, I tell myself, none of this will matter.
It will be dessicated coconut, sand dunes, you will look
and laugh at the earnest pain you once cradled and say:
was that really all it was?

But right now, torn asunder
my body a cage, a yawning lion's ribs
a dwarf rabbit's heart beating triple-time crescendo
inside the cavernous space to take up the slack
where rage has made a hearth and I can't breathe for the smoke

The future sounds pleasant,
The future is another country, it's my bones grown clean
the strain of debt, responsibility, having a nice dress for the funeral
are faint over the battle cry of Cassandra, but like every other Trojan
I take the present at face value and tell her to sit down.

Ten Hail Marys' Worth

Dear Mother,
Forgive me, for I have sinned.
I was born to it, you see: I even lied at my First Confession.
I couldn't think of anything I had done wrong, so I made something up.
I can't remember what. I can remember the guilt.
That's religion for you; it really is what you have failed to do.

I can remember the nights through that long summer where I lay awake
counting the people I had left to lose, premature mourning
a great hole in my chest left grave-open and yawning.
I can't remember how I learnt to sleep again.

But I can remember your voice on the phone,
when the slick plastic smile of coping I had so long since yoked myself to
broke like a wishbone.
I can remember you calling me an angry young woman again
and my cry-laugh
as for that one precious instant I was at our dinner table and whole.
I remember you said *we* and not *you*.

I never knew how to say thank you.
Mea culpa.

Don't fade in the telling

Tell me again the story of how we met
of how I glimpsed you perchance
or of how I hooked your eye
a Merseyside mermaid dragged in by the tide
with a witch's laugh

Tell me the story whilst we grow old
whilst we grow eternal
whilst around the moon creeps and
the moss waxes and wanes lyrical

Tell me the story
because it gives me hope that we will have a story
(that we have a story rather than a song
those three-minute one-hit wonders)
and that it will be a good one
that if we die at the end it's warm and loved in bed
so it will merely be a process of being lighter

Tell me again the story
and each time make it new
until I believe that mortals can craft their own moonlight
and make their own endings by the hearth
universes in the circles of their arms

Siren

Sing me a song of how I'm supposed to forget
what it meant to be whole.
Learn me how to forget the smell of grass rubbed into my skin
and the burn of the run, how your skin flaked under my hands and
each freckle was a kiss.
Talk me back into bed, the brace of your hands wrenching me open
and glide of my mad-girl laugh grinding me hoarse. Show me how to lick
you into silver, shiver kittenish at your mouth and
Darling, let's not lie to ourselves.
You are the most invasive surgical procedure I will ever endure.
Your petit mort eyes rob me blind. No, I don't need the anaesthetic.
Put me under.

Sweetie

Let's talk how eighteen wasn't a cherrybomb,
it was a graveyard.

It was struggling through the haze
to hear the breathing machine tick the clock down.
It was all night fasting and blood samples for breakfast and
there was no resurrection.

Eighteen was the puncture wound of a hollow wedding ring
and the tinny clap of heartbeats on the ceiling,
organs dropping like coppers, balloons deflating and

Eighteen was a personal Chernobyl
under the glitter you poured into your eyes to forget.
You brushed your teeth and taught them to smile for the funeral,
the smallness of your body and the three-patch problem
of you, a desert and a quiet death.

Let's talk how eighteen wasn't a cherrybomb,
it was a graveyard,
and you can't sugarcoat it.
It just falls off the bones.

When people say to you, you're only young once,
say *I know*
say *I figured*
think *thank God.*

Small and Insignificant Confessions

to be spoken aloud

1. I am tired of being this angry.

2. I wish I could say what I mean more often and by this I mean I wish there were parts of our lives that we could rush through, live in fast forward and by this I mean I wish there were parts of our lives that we could live in reverse and by this I mean I wish there were parts of our lives we could live in, suspended, perfect taxidermied grins stitched on our face and preserved laughter and by this I mean —

3. I long for days that slip through my fingers like sand and for the things I wish I had held onto because I used to believe you could stop the hourglass and —

1. I am tired of being this angry.

4. Yes, this is another poem whining about the gaping cavernous maw that manifests itself in the future tense. Sorrow struggles to maintain originality and so emotions are easily plagiarised.

2. I wish I could say what I mean more often and by this I mean —

5. Stop me if you think you've heard this one before, and I replay the song again and again and again and —

4. Sorrow struggles to maintain.

6. We don't speak the same language. I talk in relapse with the world always churning forward and it's hard to translate over the roar of the white noise.

7. This is the story of how you dreamed you touched him and awoke in the afternoon, glancing in the kitchen window to see glint of eyes and teeth, imagine the bones and space and alien skin and ignore the after-images haunting you to the library because after all —

6. We don't speak the same language. We never have.

8. I call you up because you tell me the world is a bleak series of exits to tell you it's not and I tell you it's not and then we talk poetry, talk all night, verse whispering from the end of the line because you are sad and prose will not reach you, warping Plath to quell the rising tide of uncertainty, a Mad Girl's Love Song to hold on when we're drowning and don't know how to ask for someone's hand, and although —

9. You won't remember this in the morning, this one time I translate myself, or I try to translate myself, transmitting a radio signal of self but —

2. I wish I could say what I mean more often and by this I mean —

2. I wish I could could say what I mean and by this I mean —

2. I wish I could say and by this I mean —

6. It's difficult to translate over the roar of the white noise.

Give blood, join Roller Derby

Psycho slut sweetheart; mahou shoujo
with little lionheart eyes and
heartbeat jewellery,
warm syrup sincerity and

You say: accessorise for the rapture.
You say: get ready to leave a pretty corpse.
You say: for me, living comes easy.
For me, this is my birthright.

I check my eyes before they roll because
I will not gun your way. The world is not manna;
God stopped volunteering when they cut the red string
tethering us together and said *there is no society,*
poured honey in their eyes and turned away.

Choke on your oyster.
My world is chronic reclamation,
painting stars and hearts over scar tissue
a process of taking back because we're all born screaming
banging against our cots for a silver spoon that never comes.
My world is learning to be enough, rough vicious girls jostling for space
joints interlinked, and this feels a little bit like love,
this feels a little bit like worship
this feels a little how champagne should taste.

I say: you know what I mean?
You don't. Don't worry.
I will not gun your way, but you'll hear the ricochet.

Anxiety Attack on Regent Street

The walk home crushes my ribcage in around me,
flatpacking me back to the factory line:
Dysfunction. Malfunction. Product recall.
I am picking out the coins for my eyes to match the wallpaper
and sealing my fingernails like armour,
a thing of talons and tar and a heart bruised up.

Ain't that just peachy. Ain't that just swell,
ain't that you dragging me through the dust in a sticky-slow suicide
and saying *isn't this nice, darling, isn't this something*
like something's better than nothing,
when actually nothing's enough,
Nothing's alright, thanks, I'm doing okay, I'm doing just fine

And the taste like warm honey in a blizzard, hair real and raven
constellations in the cradle of hips and
the key is burning through the denim to my thigh.

I don't know how to tell this story later, how to break and reshape it
to mimic the sound of laughter.

I don't know how to tell this story, how to make it sound endearing, ditzy.
Sailor Moon walking home from school, puppy-eyed and

I don't know, but why is it
in all my photographs I look like I'm about to cry?

THE LAST GREAT LOVES

1. "You and your self-mythologising again," you say. You do have a point. At least, I tell myself, I am consistent.

2. When I am eleven, I make a boy into a novel. I make the mistake of thinking the fall of his hair Byronic and attributing Keats to his eyes. In my very spine I feel that he is poetry. I get too anxious to talk to him directly, teenage performance anxiety, rely on messenger chat and talking in a room of people like it's just for him. I'm faking an intimacy he does not feel. He calls me a freak and fourteen-year-old me has never realised I could be an embarrassment to someone. It feels like gunshot. It feels like a stomach wound, acidic and insidious. Years later, he tells my friend he liked me, but he couldn't have gone out with me, of course. He says of course. She says she understands. This is the part that breaks my heart.

3. To the boy from my first date: I shaved my legs for you, even though I didn't need to, skinny jeans at fifteen, backseat cinema nerves. I held your arm at the ice rink, even though I didn't need to, my hand against the muscle of your arm, my skin against your coat and I wanted the wool gone. I smiled for you, even though I didn't need to. I smiled for you, even though I didn't need to. I smiled for you, even though I didn't need to.

4. I prise a smile from you and it drops, the penny drops, and I think oh. I think it would be so easy to love you. Spoiler: I do. Spoiler: it is.

5. When your head is on my shoulder, I can hear your heartbeat. I don't usually like listening to that, the reminder of ourselves as organic. You make it okay. You make being softer okay.

6. To the first girl I fell in love with: I saw galaxies in your eyes, the revolve of shifting colour in them when you blinked. I saw every last star in your vertebrae. You were the last gasp of a sun, an implosion of coloured synthetic silk and blood-coloured lipstick. In the end, you were something I could not touch. In the end, you were something I could not —

7. I look at your silhouette in the concert light, the Greek chorus of the music enclosing us like a strange sad womb, and I think: you are the girl my Catholic school self wanted in my future. You are the girl my teenage lonely heart hoped I would make it out the other side towards. I'm not in love with you, but you make me think of flowers. You are the other stranger in a strange land.

8. Because of you, I taught my friends about singular 'they' with all the intensity of inoculating them into a religion. I watched your face with all the fascination of the pilgrim with the icon. When you told me I was too much, it echoed in me for days, making my skeleton ring hollow. Because of you, I have carried around the weight of my own latent unspoken fear made aloud through sixteen seasons. I think I loved you, but my priest never prepared me for that. I think I want to forgive you, but though my priest drilled me in that, the words fall empty, the words fall empty. I think, I think, I think.

9. I think I wish you could have loved me back. I think I wish you could have loved me back. Our story is that we were ships in the night. Our story is that there was no story to tell. I think I wish you could have loved me back.

10. You brought me oranges. Nobody had ever done that for me before. They were the weight of a heart in my hands, and I tore them to pieces, the juice running out of my mouth, and nobody had ever done that for me before.
I could always smell the ash on your hands. I could always hear the wolves howling for meat. I could always see we weren't going nowhere, but that we were going; towards an inexorable fixed point, and I was along for the schadenfreude of it, until I remembered that's when something bad happens to other people.

11. Mutually assured destruction. Both of us holding down on the detonator, both wide-eyed as our grip grew weaker, until —

13. I can feel the expectation of a kiss growing in my chest. Your tooth catches on my lip. I walk home and wait for morning. I think this is terminal.

To The Girl I Was:

I'm sorry.

I'm sorry, I'm sorry, I'm sorry. I feel I failed you, through my own grievous fault.

I see you there, looking back across at me through the years, the memory soft and rippled, beach glass worn, and you are so young and so righteous. You are only fourteen. You do not see what is coming.

Here's what I want to tell you; let's sit down, woman to woman, because I wish I was half the woman you are, because you used to believe in what we could become, and I look to you for hope.

My spine is made of beach glass. It will withstand.

You grew up picking up stranded jellyfish to carry them back to the sea barehanded. You didn't care if it stung.

And I am not a prophet, I am not a messiah, I am a Catholic not a martyr: I am a rebel without a cause, James Dean railing at the catechism because anger is safer than admitting I don't want to believe in a God who let us down like this,

like a spiteful child refusing to clap her hands, using them to cover her ears instead, chanting I don't believe in fairies I don't believe I don't

So let's sit down, woman to woman, and here's what I want to tell you:

You will fall in love, twice, very quickly and violently, and then you'll struggle to feel like that for a very long time after. You'll tell yourself the gold dust of your love blinded you.

That's a lie.

You will spend sixteen falling into misery and the next five years trying desperately to fall back out.

Let me tell you this, my love;

and I call you my love because despite everything I do love you

though it's inconsistent and faltering, stumbling on weak legs, let me tell you this:

what those girls did to you was not your fault.

Let me tell you this:
what you have been told was wrong.

You have never been inherently bad for anyone. You are not too much. You do not poison the earth by existing.

Your spine is made of beach glass and it will not shatter.

My love, we're in this for the long haul and I will never abandon you. You are the girl who will get out of bed crying at 3am because the pain is too huge, because you take steps on ice and the ravenous sea of your sadness waits huge and black below, swirling beneath the hairline fractures. Your pragmatism will make you get out of bed anyway, scrub your eyes clean and sore, and open your textbook.

When they set up the breathing machines, you will hold your breath like they're for you. And then you will take another breath, and another.

Being alive is going to be very hard. Do it anyway.

It will not all hurt. I promise you. I am Lot's wife, a pillar of burning salt looking back to show you the way. Use me as a benchmark of how far you are from the dying city. Use me as a foothold to see how powerless the gates seem from here. I'm sorry, I'm sorry, I'm sorry. I can't give up yet.

We're going to do something extraordinary together, you and I. You just have to take my hand.

About the Author

Sarah Caulfield is a final-year Education, English, and Drama student at Downing College, University of Cambridge. She has been published previously by Lethe Press, Autonomous Press, The Mays Anthologies 22 & 24, and Voicemail Poems. She was the 2015 and 2016 winner of the John Treherne Creative Writing Prize. The eldest of two children, she has lived in the United Kingdom, Poland and Germany and is from Blackpool, Lancashire. She tweets at @holden1779

Acknowledgments

My thanks to the editors of the following publications, in which these poems first appeared:

camcreatives: "this is not" and "Don't fade in the telling" (as "Editor's Privilege")

Lavender Review: "To The Girl I Was:"

Notes Magazine: "Here To Recruit You"

The Griffin: "Rites of Passage"

The Mays: "Tallowflesh"

Voicemail Poems: "not about anyone you know"

HEADMISTRESS PRESS BOOKS

Lovely - Lesléa Newman
Teeth & Teeth - Robin Reagler
How Distant the City - Freesia McKee
Shopgirls - Marissa Higgins
Riddle - Diane Fortney
When She Woke She Was an Open Field - Hilary Brown
God With Us - Amy Lauren
A Crown of Violets - Renée Vivien tr. Samantha Pious
Fireworks in the Graveyard - Joy Ladin
Social Dance - Carolyn Boll
The Force of Gratitude - Janice Gould
Spine - Sarah Caulfield
Diatribe from the Library - Farrell Greenwald Brenner
Blind Girl Grunt - Constance Merritt
Acid and Tender - Jen Rouse
Beautiful Machinery - Wendy DeGroat
Odd Mercy - Gail Thomas
The Great Scissor Hunt - Jessica K. Hylton
A Bracelet of Honeybees - Lynn Strongin
Whirlwind @ Lesbos - Risa Denenberg
The Body's Alphabet - Ann Tweedy
First name Barbie last name Doll - Maureen Bocka
Heaven to Me - Abe Louise Young
Sticky - Carter Steinmann
Tiger Laughs When You Push - Ruth Lehrer
Night Ringing - Laura Foley
Paper Cranes - Dinah Dietrich
On Loving a Saudi Girl - Carina Yun
The Burn Poems - Lynn Strongin
I Carry My Mother - Lesléa Newman
Distant Music - Joan Annsfire
The Awful Suicidal Swans - Flower Conroy
Joy Street - Laura Foley
Chiaroscuro Kisses - G.L. Morrison
The Lillian Trilogy - Mary Meriam
Lady of the Moon - Amy Lowell, Lillian Faderman, Mary Meriam
Irresistible Sonnets - ed. Mary Meriam
Lavender Review - ed. Mary Meriam

www.ingramcontent.com/pod-product-compliance
Lightning Source LLC
Chambersburg PA
CBHW070047070426
42449CB00012BA/3180